The Rejoining of Wings

Brian Rickert Korn

Freedom is explicit because it is true

For Me

Mindful meditation kindly kindles purposeful prayer, as a man's worth is directly proportionate to his compassion and his value to his actions.

On My Natural State

Did you find God?
No
I just started to read his letters
The piled up
Wet with dust, covered
Don't be afraid of the heat
More than not
The light leans against
Resilient stamina
Unmoving
For I am moved
Away from the love of being
Brining me
Failings, faults and false freedoms
Beat the tired into losing
Slippery and bent
Mostly by my own doing
And to yours
Writing back

On joy and bravery

As it is

Prayer is inviting in something greater than yourself, and meditation is inviting the greatness within yourself

Run

Like steam: know iron and fire,
   the water knows God.
Crossing at the height of that bridge, into the city,
I
saw smoke
  being pulled like hair, a ponytail, the racing
against
planes, along
   and by the wind's
     run, running
  seems sweet like letting
      good, go. Run and
        try to undo the unknown
    pressing against
    a clay mold,
I like the face of truth's solution:
 remember
     with every gasp
     don't be disrespectful to your maker, the
devil's
demon quipped
   hardly such a thing, other than a man being
  removed from
God's hand,
           grace,

      for, forward the higher you go, the
further you fall,
                while having
something to compress
the possibilities,
            ever still temper the
panic.
    Even still the devil tolerates charity in an
empty house:
    then, when, remember
                  if your neighbors starve
you fail

God is Good

The core of you,
      as in your life,
           is God.
What a self-centered existence.
                      God is a given.
Don't return to sender
      the Lord's greatest
           gift.
God's good. Before all is through,
              he's meaning for his reflection
on
Earth to be so, too.
Her, His, Its
Happiness fills the wind.
Let this take you on Earth to the core of yourself,
being,
      all this here is vanity and worth the pains,
pleasures and partings.

Let Yourself

You alone control your breath
Your breath controls your thoughts
Your thoughts control your actions
Your actions are your value
And your compassion is your worth
We are all worth Love
Love is God
Free

Bliss

As time drips and spins
It is forever and never
Wrapped into an absence
　of nothing.
Afterwards, this binds and mixes
Into everything
That was, is and never will be
My dear,
　　　shadows squeeze
　together to hold your
　　memories lightly taught
As time drips and spins
　it is forever and never
　　wrapped into an absence
　　　of nothing

Stay close to me

Stay close to me
As you rest comfortably
You are now free
to return to boundless memories
We all shared, separately
Made fully
Gracious good deeds done
Never lost amongst the chaos
Motherly love unconditionally
A great, granddaughter, daughter, sister, niece,
aunt,
cousin and friend
Mother and wife – vowed to my grandfather's
love,
life and their
Pa and Nana's family
My grandmother
Your life well-lived, sacrifices and triumphs
abounded and held before
LoveEternal
Unconditional and True
I receive strength and hope to know
in good time, a great-grandmother-to-be in times
yet
unseen

A spirit free
I give thanks to have known, seen and love you
I love you Nana
Stay close to me
As you rest comfortably

Such

Honor God with your free thoughts, action.
For (_) is bound to timeless being.
I forgive You and me
Our journey: here to there
              then to where was when
   slow move epiphanies happened in pairs: a
 resolution of understanding and recognitions of
 grace's
fall.
Our inversion to freedom.
I love living life
    a learned lesson lines
split   open   views
Ground to sky
Let free men die
As free babies are born,
                  pulling any and all, return
    from the divine
      to this
    make the best
         of
    Earth's fleeting
  bodies faithful to living
         as long as possible
    and spirits, the same —

        transcend the conceivable
sights, sounds, and senses,
souls, the threshold
        hardly holding the other
   C'mon dude
   Beating
I am the same, until happiness depends on a home,
  such, only on
        being alone
            maintains
     claims
and reclaims
     these feelings after a good sleep.

A Lady Says

We are more alike than different
Don't be indifferent
Worse than ignorant
For no one's benefit
To hold bad temperament
Love jubilant
Be thankful permanent
It's commitment
I am a serpent
A faculty of excrement
Purge that department
Be gone torment
I see den Horizont
We are more alike than different

Blackhearted

Her eyes unwound before me
Staring directly at my head
But my heart
Wickedly seeping
Retreating
That's what they said
I agreed too much at least
Simple
A moment here
A broken heart there
Madness and pain
It had nothing to do with my head
But my heart
Needed time away from
This hell freezing by
    numbed breath without air
As energy flickered
My fallen gut tore
No I say
I am not
A little white
A little red
A little truth
Goes a long way

Love's Progress

Love surrounded Hate and won
Love surrounded Fear and won
Love surrounded Ignorance and won
Love surrounded Prejudice and won
Love surrounds You
Your Love surrounds Me and is winning

If there is

An emptiness to fill
Or a condition to settle
The latter sounds more like it
Not something to fill up
But to share with
This is no interlude
Between solitudes
It takes a multitude
To comprehend the magnitude
    You feel this emptiness
A fullness to spread
Or an understanding to regret
The former sounds more like it
Not anything to take from
But to give to

Muck

I saw a shooting star last night
Lasting the opening of my smile
Shading the shadows
Across the deck
A net for the splitters
;) sanguine
    instead of the arrival
The ships turning the ships turning
Turn the ship
It's really us isn't it
Painting the walls as these halls flounder

Origami

In this
Living for the next
Perpetual spacing
Get the being lauded
And censure things like
Regretted anticipation
Ha, what if they weren't
Anymore
Our pliable luck
These bodies of origami

All this from

A feeling of stormy eagerness
Become something
That is
For every last drop
That is
Becoming something
Hold shaded lakes to
A feeling of stormy eagerness
Resets ebbs flows
Towards an about face
That is
Becoming something
Become something
Rock rhythming
By light cracks over water flows
That is
A feeling of stormy eagerness

And then

Here lit by slits
Melodic bushels
Of thin slivers
Hung high
In the kaleidic movement
Ruptured by a gold freshness
Strongly propped on
The wind's edge
These diamond vibrations
Allow my gaze to lift wide
Through to here, where
A blush sky holds the cat-eyed-sun
There are lines stretching
A beam down the center
There rising with steady speed
An expanse of a moment
There are layers, too
A silence away from
There to elevate this
A glimpse of creamy red on skin
There she stares boldly
A calmness in her eye
Turns those dark water leaves
    to frame a rust-dust-moon
Hooked by the sky
Perched and centered
A silhouette of sorts to its backside

Opening to the blackness and pin-cut-light
I see this
Marvel a bit
Press my lips
And head indoors

Nothing but

I listen to the gospel when I celebrate and hear it
when I struggle

These are but the best
Seemingly to be settling
I recognize the game
And don't want to play
Existing sounds like
Giving everything away from all this bullshit
to sealed letters and falling rain

Passing

Followed up by
   my indigestion with the world
   were the in-between of days
Rounded to the backside of consequence
A gaping mouth, adding perspective,
   leaking the suck of something good
This time, hope muted a bit more
   next to the silent lots of cowards
   deserving of life's howling
Its naked world sounds
   bubbling louder than
   my indigestion with the world

So with this

Let's all be here right now
In this shared experience
I want to recognize
Your family, we are where you are from
Your friends, they reflect your sides
And your bride, she mirrors your heart
Between the beats and blessed stillness of breath
She is with whom you share love
With whom you will share your life
Afterwards and before
This here is a moment
That will bind the movement of purpose
Between these two
Their pull of love has just become an honest union
Vulnerable and fiercely
Tried, true and between these two
They see each other
They have chosen each other
To love, to defend and raise above
For one, and I know for all here
The two of you have given us reason to celebrate
You have given us opportunity to give thanks
And to see that this day is wonderful and good
This is the point of everything we do

A Struggle of Sorts

Literally crazy
And profoundly correct
I've heard what you've done
Never saw it though
Can't say I know
About
This
But I'm starting to feel
So I'll just go with the flow
And let be
Something
Literally crazy
And profoundly correct

Loud Focus

We should go back
Through the mist
Between the trees
To where light
   blankets over stridden paths
I should go back
  to where I've been
On leveled ground
 with sheets of
  nowhere
Between the mountain top
And this shallow ditch
You should go back
Not then here
Emergency's gentle appeasement of things,
      unsettled, pops my sight to fever
Brings me back
My sweat blends with the water-soaked air
around
It drags me towards
    my drier eyes to gain loud focus on the
      staggering journey ahead

I rest my head

She said
I lied flat with the Earth
In that span that I don't remember
I was asleep
Her dog woke me as I jerked up
There was soft momentum from the dog,
   happy to have found something
  in this bed of grass
I wasn't seen by her, distracted, perhaps
    by her limp
And now, the sun moved below the trees
Green darkening
It is, as I am under the Earth's follow,
      over and beyond,
   ready for my night

The In-between of Days

Nothing to suck air through aching teeth
No numbed-out stomach

Your feelings won't stop
So, don't worry about the front side on this done deal

Soon enough
We'll all thank god we didn't have nothing

Next Door

You had a dream last night
As we slept together
Sitting in this beer drenched church
Next to the perverted altar
You told me
There was a door
The devil in-between the threshold
Closed in by horns and open flesh
Click – the cavernous hall shrunk
    and my eyes fluttered around memory
He called to you
Yes
Said I needed
Something familiar to me
Terror grabbed my gut
From your lips this hurt
Confusingly
An accurately acute past prophecy
Lingered between sips
About every other thought
Good
Slippery wet, bent
Determined patience keeps that shut
My back against the pounding

Schwerkraft

Ich bin ein Mann
Keine Angst hab' ich
Sondern Traurigkeit
Überwältigt und hart
Vergiss nichts von Alles
Ich bin hier
Für eine Zeit
Und für immer
In diesem Herz
Schwebt die Liebe
Zwischen meinem Atem
Und unserer Luft
Lass uns tanzen
Die Musik spielt wahr
Von der Hoffnung
Viel Rhythmus hab' ich
Ich bin ein Mann

Sind aber Gleich

Gott sei Dank die Gedanken frei sind
Ohne zu sehen, nicht aufgeben
Breit ohne Platz
Liebe ohne Bedeutung
Die Natur bildet mir was ein
So gottlich wie möglich
Besser als nichts
Und nichts ist besser
Vielleicht doch dein Kuss
Sind aber gleich

The Swell of Things

Things are a removed beauty
With ashes' strokes of color
Where I follow
Around my shoulders and back
Elevate
With head heavy posture

Body leaps
Draw jagged sweetness
From stops and tries
A victim plays your eyes into dryness
But hunts vicious, validating and varied
    to their own degree
Behold the swell of things
Caused by this hateful love

This Choice

She wrote letters
So they would be ok
With what she gave away
Then she bought more scarves
Just a trim and no follow-up
I'll see you soon and help with the door
She bought more and bathed herself with cloth
The oozing of skin wasn't what she wanted
She wanted
To make it to Christmas
Decidedly
Everyone celebrated early that year
Her second last premature came quick
And she died later than they thought
Her friend volunteered that she'd know when
She certainly did
Do well
Not as a coward
And was ready for this to be
Everything
But easy
When starts to slip into spinning

The Truth of It

Life is so hard
Yet so good
You should know that
It gets better
This, however, is up to you
Open up and let it in
Break down these
Walls and barriers of weighted
Hurt, sorrow and pain
As moments of lightness return
Wait for it
Seek it
And love it
Open up and let it in
From alone desperation
And broken cries
Breathe through to
Our extended hands
And strong beats of
Hope
Open up and
It gets better
Life is so hard
Yet so good
Open up and let it in
A trickled drop at first
It will come

Wait for it
Seek it
And love it
Be here with us
As it gets better

Turn it off

I'm sure you see it, too
Though limited
Belonging to contorted obedience
This particular sight
The heavier side of humankind
Does start to stretch here
With on demand circus
And high fructose bread butter
Crowded around and recorded

I watch this here in third person
Once removed from
Too much life
Without
Living

What it is

What lives here
    is circumspect, erase
The only sound
    pretend
    brain tremors
    heart quakes
    shifting bones
passing breath

To the Bone

Fill my hands
These are strong
Built to carry, lift
I want them rough
Wash these hands with purpose
Built to pull, hold
Make them learn through struggle
Let them mold the solution,
    smooth the resistance,
    and comfort the pain
Allow them to praise, mend and
    crease with age
Shake them without malice
My hands are open

Presumably

Papal piety's prevailing prejudices and persecutions
Preside over perverted predatory postures
Pages pour past and present with presumably
   pardoned pleasures
Posing, publicly perplexed at perceptions of
   pathetic, putrid,
      pigeoned preachings
Perpetually protected in private to prey on purity's
   promise
Personal pride promotes political pathogens to
   plague profusely

People protect people in Providence
Proper prudence and purposeful prayer prevent
   pointless pain
Pointed pistols or prophetic poetry, padre?
Please prepare to pay profoundly and permanently

Look Up!

The water lines flicker above
As they travel down and across
Look up!
These little water beads stretch out
Over skin, hair and cloth
Look up!
They dribble down my brow
And trickle my goosebumped shivers
From my grounded happiness
Look up, I say, look up!

Backhanded

When words fall apart
  to removed existence
And follow though undoings
  still the undone
In a wallowing stance
Slower than thought
Stop
And readjust expectations

I think the rhythm will save us
No matter what
A tight held hand
Tremors back
From the not-always-about-me
Let be
Truth's simple embrace
Echoing behind this wind-struck face

Loved

And now
It is sung
With raw tones of gravity
Accenting this hurt
Arranged with squeezed partings
Wrapped in the constriction of now
Death's frozen life's last
Round of discomfort
This pain chaps my breath
And empties my chest
My eyes fill wet
As my voice cries
A silence of sorrow
Pulls me apart
Weakened by distance
From you lying there
Being as close as my hand
And now, away forever

What is God?

What do you need God to be?

Perfection

The pull of dawn
Waiting on a breach of senses
A bottomless high
To something built up
Worked for
Quickspecs
And centered pleasure
Repeat
Nothing as good as the last
Or better than now
A truth
A release
A use
Pushed away
Compounding problems combined into perfection
Now, wait
        to show absent happenings of lateral
  sweeps

Little Bouts

It's all about
This or that
That if this
Control projected
The downward avalanche of chance
With rechecks, adjustment and repetitions
So
Now what about
This or that
That if this
Steady these thoughts
In your head
Make it click
Back
Just going for one more time's
Bout of compulsion
Away from what
It's all about

A Glance

Leaves collect a still life, among other things
Dew, cracks and veins wind throughout
Chaos slips through your fingers, and this petite
bird
  with youthful eyes chirps light
                            voiced in a small
  framed world

Linger Loved

This will be hard
And this will be sad
A dignified parting would be nice
What happened to old me dying?

This prolonged avoidance inches,
  visit by visit, my me towards
  burden and pity
    The passage of an elder evokes
  sober respect, I do think:
    A life well-lived
    Admired by lucid ones
    Needed
    Loved
There are worse things than dying, you know

Heartless chaos shouldn't upset
        maternal rhythms, and didn't here
    He was a good man
Respect is deserved and so is rest

  I go away, gently drifting beyond to
            the center of your hearts

This Guy

You need a mirror
To do that
So I can see where it goes
When did it become this for you?
Slow
Lies
Fully
I gave up
Haven't found
He got stuck
Well, not really
But it's hard to leave
The middle of fine
1 to 10
No talking
Have a cigarette
Give me a number
And leave
Or die
It's all good
This is the work
And this is your life
Meaninglessly
Look at this
Undone, wounded into testing, festering and
Holy shit
You just shot in your neck

Decent Dunces

The delirium of the divine
   divides and decides the do's and don'ts
     of decent dunces

Bread and Butter

I got a workout that night
Hunting to be caught
The here and now
Slowly sounds
Like the failing of morning
Often does
Pushed to the center of me
Comfortably folding
Into the wicked side of ordinary
And first it happened
   then tomorrow slipped
Just like that, once
With exponential growth
Dividing through attachment
An action tally
Quotas
Complete
And repeat
Fill us up
Until the white stuff comes
These hearts were all but black
We mostly stop being
Quite honestly
Men
Humanity is quite to the contrary?
Raw and wicked
Time starts to end when

I look at me, you and him

Even a demon is a bit repentant, reluctant and rash
   in recovery
      and after a defeat is not the time to regret
   forfeiting
Lasting about a generation
Now more lost
Before the next time came
    to stop
    and become decent men of a certain persuasion

Again and Again

United we stand
Divided we fall
And united we stand up
United we wait
United we push and pull
United we are different
You and I fall
And united we stand up, again

Chalk

There was never much to leave behind
The wore
Hung on his face
Like frozen agony

Masterpiece

(intended to be read under the shade and over tea from publications of notable narrative, bzw. the top-down-funneling of what is worthy verse, a la the New Yorker or whatever)

------Page Over------

Pretentious

This

Entire eternity
   of
Waves and waters
   Pulls out perfection
Brining me back
   to
Waves and waters

Done

A permanent continuing
The crowds, recently have dwindled
By, but, because
   we have to do something, having
 a path
The nature of people continues with less
predictable
 Hey, describe yourself
Remember you, too, in respect to them
Those that are not yet here, will not know today.
Our
space
   continues on, I pray, supposing, this being
 those beings stopped, their halts disappeared
   into a permanent continuing

Just the Moon

The cold cuts deep as it rides the wind
The gangly treetops sway, blocking momentarily,
      the faint, sparse stars above
The moonlight pulls the hard, let-be
      ground where I stand by a
      cluster of winter's flower-buds
The memory's whisper of the sun lines my jacket,
      but the bellows of bluster burn my exposed
      ankles – no socks tonight
The cigarette is now long out, blackening my
      fingertips in this shimmering night-light
The time to go in has come. One last look up at the
      moon reminds me I should have worm
      a heavy coat

Waving Cloth

Drum drum
Beat beat
Move your feat soldier
We'll cut you down
And then you bury them up in
Acknowledged, ignored and prioritized
Responses, numbness and shutdowns
Things to be
Things have seen
Things we do kill the living
Ignorance is bliss
Shit is shit
And spun carnage looks fine
          against waving cloth
A roundabout way of saying
Drum drum
Beat beat
Move your feet soldier
Nothing to see here
Life is not equal
Undo this misfortune
Bury bury
You know it is ok soldier
If you can't
It's ok
This is your night
Your night before

It's ok
You've done well
At least you did your job
All a man can hope to do
Drum drum
Beat beat
Move your feet solider
Bombs drop
Scattered lots of pencils and paper
Soaked through and through
Hard work and leaflets of regret
Comfort no blackened skin
Happenstance, serendipity and coincidence
Rubble tears in folds
Making the wash of time
More naked and loud
It is cold on these streets
Of well-intended targets and
      forsaken obscenity
Drum drum
Beat beat
Move your feet soldier
To the winner's trot
He she them
We have won
Without a doubt
Another war

This always happens

When you estrange yourself from hope, because of
her ever diminishing offerings and returns, just let
her atrophy, and while she is regrouping, build
something

like the bible reminds me of nuclear power, for its
knowledge, applied with collective, selective
responsibility, could make everything so much
better, yet without prudence, it ignites hell on
earth

and for some, an accepted mix of awareness and
empathy, can lead to brilliant doings and
devastating
understandings that undo an honesty, then a
failing,
whose end is just that – a certainty worth the
extension, though

Breaks

Bold banners bound in blood
Bring back burned bodies and
        beautiful bounties
Break
Bottles bang bursting with brew
        and bubbles
Babies are born
Break
But bottomless blues brings bleak
        blackness because
Bold banners bound in blood
Bring back burned bodies and
        beautiful bounties
Break

A Fond Memory

It is a hot night, and I am dry
These stairs seem to be too steep
Not too crowded, good
People moving all around on this sticky floor
I see one, dancing to the rhythm
The same one I'm feeling
His perfect eyes dart towards me as I slide across
We connect, he smiles, looking down his
        shoulders
Mirroring the music so gently
The lights prance around his inviting look and
        expose his beautiful, open torso – sexy
His scent travels across my face and I want more
That one, get to know him
Digits exchange through crowded blackness of the
        lined back
The air around you is sweeter than…anything
But I want more than a taste, more than a touch
I want to wake up every morning to those
        at-first-sight eyes and that sweet
   nectared air of your kiss

On the falling

Letting it be
Let it be reflected in the memories of others'

Worth the pass you by lookbacks and leanings
To stop
Suspension's safety
Lying beneath
Held tight sights
Scrapes the suck of different views
Besides, aside from the haves and the never-wills
Deafening warmth
Spreading out into
Naked world sounds
Meant for other's fall of absence
After the quiet rests muted
On so much love

Hey
Our eyes connect
And circumvent
Why we're all so fucked up
The corners of luck and such
Divide the pick ups
Lit up sped
Not just only dead

The lights there

Showing the good, the bad
And the point of a being so tired
Now, just try to break the fall of others

The Day After Good

Swallow these words, insufferable
Ourselves, sly and steady
Construct the raw
I say
Why not rivet the up
Nimbly striking the laziness of proofs
Let's talk about what
What was that?
She wrote about once
It stopped the until now
From what's ignoble
   letters and fiction
      surface of rising and
         the light of, what what
 was untaken from free
 writing
Shaken into goodness
That quick response silence
Within
I take heed from me, to, ah, these
Please
Sacrifice the now
For your tomorrow
I guess there's morning
Tomorrow is a good day to be born
During the in-between of days
I am born for tomorrow

Let Her Be Now

There is silence in the ashes
I believe there is peace
The Bell Tower rings on the hour
And more often will I remember
How it once was
Before we are here
In the center of our hearts
When we were
That sound of wind
Thrusting life from above
Still firmly
We are the ones who remember
The ones who hurt
Let us hold the sorrow
In the stains and streaks on our cheeks
Between us there is nothing but
Love
Now, leveling the void
       of her being
Gone and still there
Firmly in joy
And forevermore
Free

What I ask

dance for love
dance for life
dance for us
dance for you
dance for your enemy
dance for your forgiveness
dance for your family
dance for peace
dance for art
dance for beauty
dance for knowledge
   for you to dance around hatred
 so that not
       even the slightest ignorance or evil
      has a place in your heart
dance with God

Pathos

When does the post come, sir?
After the game is done,
  my fellow son.
Let us both strive to earn its delivery

With Where

Faith ignites alongside forgiveness
Lead, tin and copper
Smolder the incredulity of believing
  plain sights and naked sounds
These tie the ribbon
With where the end of our sun
Sets for an embrace
More than yourself
Bronzed and bathed
I see you
And after looking that way
To where
More in faith
Than in sorrow
I am free

The Sound of Ice

The rub of dirt smoothing on skin
The sound of movement when ice forms
The different planes, the sky and the sun
    I stayed, just past there.
Love yourself, and the rest will form around you
                                            us
                                           them
                                      we

stayed
    just past there, the undercarriage of clouds

                                                  (End)

                Time faded into dates,
        shrinking behind forgetfulness.
                  The pain nestles

The Pressure of Stone

> The horrors of hate
> The failings of fools
> The consequences of
>   complacency

Are a simple summary, an alliterated list, which speak to how we falter.

    Like the word 'Action' inscribed into cement, just by an extended finger, over and over again, I know you understand these set-aside truths, too.

Even if the pressure of stone doesn't weigh down your doings.

The Roll of Revelations

The resolution sets inward,
   to the sun behind the clouds. On a wet day
the weight of your bread is
substantial
Let's get fed.

_____

_____Faith, like Forgiveness, is a daily

Choice and Joy

_____

You were never able to grab hold of the water, so
we'd change the temperature from time to time.
What a horrible catch-all. What a net.
    When your rock-bottom becomes your
ever-shifting surface, you're in some deep shit.

Whiskey Talk

Around the table or corner of a bar, a campfire, the
beach. The place doesn't matter, instead what's said

      anger, dread, uncouth, shaken, breathless
  shock, crass and rough, funny stuff
    my bigoted puss

     popped

A dry-drunk or shit-faced fucked-up
My tongue, uncovered and confided, flowin' 'cause
 of this hard stuff, real gruff. Ha

After the drink is drunk, shared and thrown-up
I'm better and more in-touch
  as to my I wake up
And super glad we hand this private talk

Mourning (_) God (_)

So, I was like: I love god. And miss god. I'm mourning God in celebration of all that was provided, inspired and extended to me by grace, mercy and spirit. I live. God and I have said goodbye.
I am now just me upon the release of Thee
          (oh geez, omg – blaaah)

And then

    I was in hell.

    – ehh, welp –

Thanks for keeping the door open, God

Good, lol z

Flutters, Bristles and then

The sound steady

    calms the loss of love,

  fondly screaming

    heart heavy, beyond all senses and sense.

 Now and then, just running on a reaction to faith,

     not shared by the living.

I am free

    to release reality's removed relationship to

right,

     realizing the relevance of relating.

And then, I come again to hope, understanding

apathy

    to be more estranged than the underpinnings

of why we tear ourselves apart.

        We tend to the running of our in-between.

As they were, the experience of things done,

    doesn't mean it ain't what it is — everything, but

the truth.

Here, is where the before

  afterwards
        transpires into then

Religion

Religion is a handicap for the spiritually stunted? Kind of: a poor man says 'just power structures of political control over the masses' and a wise man says 'help is good like that within communities, traditions and family – keep them close'. Yep.

And so, if religion is the opiate of the masses, then faith is the freedom.
    Faith is like a stone – set and settled – amongst the
      waters of wanting.

Honestly

On this Earth,

in the quiet of reflection,

the standard disposition of any
informed and decent adult is
depressed,

so raise me up with art, love and work.

And because of everything,

I give thanks.

Click

Tree Rings

And then the sky looked back
And I found God in the meantime
The moon emoted tree rings
In the milky grey light
A halo
Just everywhere a full moon a circumference
Like water breaks under soft mist
The inverse told the truth

Luck is just universal vibes making a bet that you will
start earning your success soon enough, with encouragement and a card trick or two ;)

Carpe elmothafuckin' Diem

Aren't we all pawns in the memory of our history?

Smoke rose in angles like a ballon cresting the cuts and fires in my heart, hopefully as before, when your kiss tempered the kindling of us

The coming fall

Bows, arrows and patchwork shadows
Backlit with creases and holes
Around sliver lips, open, in rocked faces
Tightening against bobbing ferns
These evergreen dances
Avoiding the great fall, once again
Our flaking trees offer down the ready
       for next season's gains
Teamworked and piled
Hisses sprang from buzzing rain
Hitting the leaves
So they'd chase each other
All the way to the flat piles
      of cozy yellows and fire-set orange
Some meandering
Some in tandem
Some darting
Layered wet
And piecing together to cushion the ground
       for the fall of what is to come

Better off than biting

Tinted gums distract from a crooked posture
Perpetually ignorant of nothing less, as those
  big eyes shift for more than an approving glance
Watch it dear, you may fall out of that top
Respect
Times aren't changing
Cement earrings dangle throughout
There is something of a flutter in her voice, just
  just like sandpaper
My rational fears project onto her face, wait,
  that's just me, she smiles more than I laugh, and
what's that? Just happiness we hear, all the pride
in herself hugs the air when talking about how
her baby is great and good, really good

On the fly

    Bounded in ball on the floor with
    one pair of ripped jeans that keep you
    warm in
    cold showers
You rob houses and do drugs
What else?
Oh, preserving innocence, he says
What took yours?
You're a good kid with a shitty life
Grimy music echoes around you, bouncing off your
    tired eyes right back at me
I see you, but what
Hmm, this little prince sits alone, drowning on the dock
    I bet you could slalom well, catch a beer on the
    fly and   then jump the wake
I'd shake my head if you got seasick
Don't think you would, though

You might be a handsome, fucked-up man one day,
    despite any luck

This day you take cold showers, and sit in a ball on the floor,

your eyes cast down at your ripped jeans,
knowing fully,
and too soon, that your life is not for living

Loves

A lover's love, a rush of riverfall
A beloved's love, a deeply triumphant mountain
A friend's love, a sweet and rolling field
A sister's love, a curling and echoing of tides
A brother's love, a thick and sturdy forest
A father's love, a grounding for the stance of trees
A mother's love, a breadth beyond oceans

God's Love – playfully dwarfs the expanse of stars,
   lights circle and smile back, covering, cheering,
   lifting the life of ground and ocean

Vice Quota

Ain't nobody love me
Ain't nobody care
Pounds down – hard led

    Comfortable here
    Slight pain keeps my balance
    Steadying these hands, suspended
    Over quilts of boredom
    The piled years repeat
    Folding into when
    We bring the rhythm
    Clapped into nothing held back, lacking
    High sets of us by ways

Clustered rhymes and cushions of truth, make do
The wicked, self jump drive intercept

    Heavy forehead
    Repeated actions
    Etched out ends
    Means and circumvent
    The point of our
    Bread and circus
    Keep us from naked world sounds
    Pick up habits
    Stay below ground
    Talk to me aloud and lose your

Vice Quota
Hold my shame abreast
And all the rest irrelevant
Ain't nobody love me
Ain't nobody care
Pounds down – hard led

I see me and just wallow in despair

Timing

This folly of a passion covers the whole of my heart
As straddled shutters move my blood warmly throughout
Responsive skin gives with pressure
And tight posturing couples the gently rounded,
        handfuls of flesh
A masculine dusting collects hot effects in soft folds
While parted thrusts slide towards comfortable repetition
Ever aware, readjusted rhythms prolong avoidance of
        coming solitude
This rebounded love

The Dawns

Sprayed rose petals explode out oils awash on canvass
Yellow-tipped gold lines trim the edges
As shadowed pink clusters arrange against forest greens
Wood wrapped marble supports this
An old, dying man's rhythm of things robs me blind of
        these views
It was the best of times

No more sunrises
No more twilight's mist, gray spattered air falling along
        glowing beached shores
I sit among the waved licks
Saltwater arises out of the blackness
This punctures my sensibilities, as life hinders one's
    living, and compels him to capture
    what is held in these four corners

Driven

Wayward motion lifts bent elbows as persistence
                leads throughout
Turning head
Brisk movement on two feet,
      arms lead the way
A veil of frowned-out skin drapes over bones of roses
     and metals
Destination forward
 Vacuumed locked affairs lurk behind a mask of
 feigned protection, sitting just below her mouth
While straps strike against black haired tightness
Transient, like ghost
On her way, on her way

Reflected

I want myself
    how sound waves pierce time together,
    growing slower with quickening pace
Perception is earned
A hallow picture frame lays against a broken door,
    casting sloped angles across the tan, wood
    paneling
Up from the floor, I see visions of unified shading
    supporting, bracing an image to add color
    within our hallway of familial wrinkles,
    captured like stone on shadowy paper

That sounds good – a life
A measure towards fine
Life lingers through my veins, as the undulation of
    memories rescues me from the threshold
    of evil, once again
Stop
Hear those sound waves returning after the
darkness
    gives purpose to the light
Prostrate these texts and bury myself throughout
    these words
My voices vibrates, elating my knowledge of a
    life well-lived

Come Never Again

Separation grows steady
    against a Winter's draped tree
Lumbering treetops support
    a heavy, grey-cast sky
You aren't here, always there
In the morning you escape me
Why do you leave?
These distances prickle my heart
It's not unbearable, after awhile
Our love smolders along treaded paths,
    slowly melting away on these winding
        stretches
I love you so much I want to leave
I want to push away your strong hands,
    push against your hairy chest,
    keep you a-far
I want to turn from your soft lips, framed by
    full-bearded grin
Avoid your eyes
I was just honestly truthful

Naked Skin

The air dropped
I sat up in bed
And wanted to die
Before our night stopped
You told me you've known for a long time
Darting to the bathroom
I stayed upright
Hearing you dry heave in the dark
It was cold, like that time I gave everything away

The air dropped
Before you left the bed
Darting to the bathroom
I let myself lay heavier into the sheets
And tried to blend into my blank eyes more
You told me you've known for a long time
I recalled bad acting, wicked conspirings and
      irrelevant judgment
I heard a void of silence
As you dry heaved
It was cold, like that time I gave everything away

My Water Spot

The water pricks
When the skeeters let go of light grips
It's pretty like this
Ribbons and ripples
Sort of balance on top
As a quick-dart mosquito hovers above
Waiting for the next yum yum drop
Or is it a hearty gulp
Tunneling apart the shadows
      amidst the greens that fill-up
          our creek bed-top
The sun softens here
Ready or not

Success

Make happiness
Work for blessings
That's real success
Leave the mess
Where it belongs
Under, to the sides
Or hard efforts
With this bliss
That is mine, yours
And ours
Make happiness

Ownership

These there are mine unfortunately
These sharp lines of sickness
These are created from less-than-goodness
These solid and varied with degree
These are cut-blood-bounded
These are pink with creamy edges faded
These are red with gloss shiny
These are pointed towards newness
These stretched triangles of despair
These here belong to me

Heads will roll

Boom shakalaka
Boom shakalaka
Boom!
I'm not good at basketball
It's just, sometimes, I get lucky
Swoosh
Heads will roll
A quick release from the hand, limp-wristed
Faggot
What do you want me to be?
I'm one step behind you
You set the pace, my friend
Do you feel better?
What do you want me to be?
You are so forgettable
Wait! We're not done yet
That's it, let the blood drip from your mouth,
      over your lips
It's sweet isn't it, like licorice
And that is a good thing
Don't be afraid or eat with your mouth full
Relax your throat, limp-wristed,
      blood-red lipped
Now you can talk
Tell me everything
Faggot

Schoolin'

Fill it up
Rattle rattle
Fill it up
Click clank
This jar here
You see it
Release your hand
Rattle rattle
Click clank
Let it go
Up in the jar
And drop!
Well done!
Click, clank
Now, child, tell me your reasons

Every Good Day

The dukkha sowed settled into the soil,
    where his knees
           found grounded happiness,
    extended and ready, beyond
the sky,
       with the help of wind,
    on his way home, high fiving the Divine

What if the world is God's eyes, looking back at 'us' into
these mirrors, our hearts and those eyes?

The Pass of Perfume

Time to share into the picture you're taking, so you can
see my eyes look off-set from center, make study
of them and be set like circles. I'm laying down in
fault's lives and love's redundancies. You write
papers and sit comfortably, as the eyes linger
in printed ink. I hope you get a good mark
constraining reality, and a good
send-off, erasing yours.

If I stay in this moment

  I'm good here, well

    what's coming is there

      over to the next moment,

        movement, mine.

The Names of Stone

    lilac and lavenders

like quilted water on stream

  woven ripples and smoothed crests

    on the other side of hues and heaving

(In) Bursts of Laughter

Emanates loud gently
From this one
Fully of Love
And closest to your two hearts
New among us
Conjuring the cause just by
Here is Life a new
Among us
And from
A blessing, a laughter, a love
From you two
Your gift (in)to the world
And to you, too
From the Highest Above Love

Generally and Specifically

Them the other whom has received your hate
Is in God's hands, too
Pray for the me in you, like the inverse I do, too, is
    in us, universally and through
The coming of fools is often late to realize,
    we all lay down, separately,
   the same way our own,
before our Maker

What's in the middle of nothing bad and everything good?

Life :)

Taking a seat

I was scratching the surface of a table, when
really, I
was simply invited to sit presently

What God Allows

And the Lord
Wet leaves and eyes
Instincts and mornings
Goodbye's and first light's gaze
Warm tears
And Thank You's
Rest
A mother's praise and grievances
Sorrow and regret
Patience and virtue
Forgiveness and forward
A birth and first breath
Our kiss and clicks, cracks and whispers,
          inches, our roar's flight
And thank you's until the Morning comes
We exhale and intake the knowing when
   to fall
Freely
Given and soaring
Love's home's whistles
And Hope's love

Affirming miracles

Hope, Hurt and Horror

My hope and hurt
    are deeper than the bedrock
I dig and push. I lift my arms and hands and force my
    brow up and up
  deeper!   deeper!
      What a joy!

My pain

My horror lays shallow on perceptions of permanence,
me forgetting in fear, that I can't do anything or
everything that I do, or don't, has no effect on the coming
of tomorrow, so whether I am there or here,
then or now, a part or not

Plain and simply the curved bedrock, with layers yet
unseen, sing and sings a preview of tomorrow's majesty, our
      daughters and sons

When you don't hate, you are free.

Over the water

The dock shakes and waddles by the Bell Tower,
the dragonflies mate, the boats' wakes tilt the
 hauls up – the waves, bobbing over butter, glass
  and water

7/4/2017

 The music banged
 The bones protruded
And no birds sang
 The music banged
 The bones protruded
And no birds sang
 The music banged
 The bones protruded
And no birds sang!

The Quartet wondered about nothing.

And death was surely set, that this was hell

(Here) ---

Laughter and hiccups
The oblivious youth yells back and laughs
The petulant children whine
While sometimes
The adults draw their mouth corners tight
 against their cheeks – a grin would be too
  right – since, we are all greased with
 burgers and fries and meat, like the deeds,
 the decadence, the decisions we take and
 make, right

(There) ---

A fence kept them in, while life kept them out
               of living, of laugher, of love

(Here) ---

In paradise, I write this sharply aware of failings,
of fight and of famine from freedom
               there where their music banged
against
bones: men and women and children and the old,
murdered, and death, not yet them, but
suffered living

      My breathing and sight stopped, my pen
turned between my fingers, and my hand grips,
 now my brow condenses above my thoughts
get

      shocked, the bird song, back to here
                    in Paradise, where this
and now,
just thinking, and while
  thinking of their lot,
    that when and where their music
  banged their bones to rot,
      another when and where the birds
  cried tormentedly,

helplessly watching
   kin kill kin
  cursing, cursing
    your horrors of Humanity!!!

Wanderings of Daylight

The tightening of history and the catch up of afternoons
We're all angry, aren't we?
    Life predictably brushes away screams
        to joys performed like well sung blues
    smooths
Ha!
The conditioning of culture
There is great revelry in manipulating the truth:
    just about
        that youth live wildly for freedom,
        while adults die willingly for liberty.

It's better this way, they say
Like chops on a block, or something like you
Searches for inspiration in the quiet of afternoons

Light of day

The doubled down sun on the river and sky,
    as to sanctify this day's run.
I paced myself, and drew an equator,
        as I ran along the water, pacing myself,

        drawing an equator from the flecked

        bubbles leveling off to when I saw in the

        flow, in that I belong. There, I am down by

        the river, going on my way,   as the

            birds called back

                the light of day

Use

But I exist with
   the bendings of faith

 Before my breathless deep stopped

    and showed hard ways of shutters and blows.

But I exist with.

My breath is dry from use

Thanks, for coming

    over with the abuse's damp and gnarly sounds.

I got over the shadows' loudness, and the views

The only rain that came was a drip from the air conditioner. And the smell was overwhelming, less eclipsed by the use of existing, the condensation and drops.

When

Prayer works when you do

    Rejoicing, regrouping and reducing

    Times hard lucked

Weighed down by crisscrossed sand

Prayer works when you do

Gratitude fills thanks full

Courage and clarity

Prayer works when you do

Yourself and Everything

Because
God said to listen
And then God said to hear
And God said to hold
And then God said to mourn
And God said to have courage
And then God said to cry
And God said to breathe better
And then God said to keep
And God said to die
And then God said to see everything
And God said try, again
And, God, I said I hurt
And then God said to watch
And God said to me, too
And then God said to hope
And God said to heal
And then God said to lay it down
And then God said to liberate
And I said gladly

Seeing the Other

      the rapture and rubble
        the ridicule

      the rejection of right

      the redundancies from

        the dead of night

            such is life:

(American) Life exists after the rapture's drop. I wonder if

that's just for me – who else sees the reasons behind

such framed living?

The others, too.

My friend

Only birds in the sky,
black mostly, with visible beaks,

the young and blue, and sun-soaked through.

Heart

love yourself

stronger

than the pain

hurts you

Reconciling belief and life takes grit and might,
and lots of luck. The I in me might make sense of
all this

drunken Belief or sober Faith

a mixed drink sounds more like it

since Easter seems like

every time

some body

turns zero

What happened to you?

Life, my son

Else what's the point in all this madness and such naked world sounds?

Around the Corner

The angels, a continuous clapping of conversation
in the crowd,
slightly tight and taught sounding

in thank you's

The war of there

"get up, get up, get out of there!" he hollered too calmly for it being, "too hot to lie down in that", "get up" kept falling out his open mouth, from where the screams and strings of spit had nowhere to go but down, over his cracked and purple lips, as the dry skin and long scruff, grey and uneven, was also covered in mucus, which mostly fell and hit the sandy ground, for the soil was just dirt, like his pointlessly endless circle of toil was soaked through between his broken shoes; the bloodied Earth was gasping and his son had died, and now, couldn't get out of there

Traffic jams and more

Such simple implications
    Do you ever count the cars or acknowledge

    the stars and such divine laws,

like the expanse of heavenly Love?

And your duty to radiate and reflect, despite

the worst prospects and bests?

    The nakedness of forgiveness

Remember the equilibrium of waves has a moment

longer than its break, while the twinkle

of stars in the night has a sight reflecting back at You

Such simple implications

Remember, we are guests here

Upside-down and backwards

He cried with the rain that day
Upside-down and backwards
Over and over again, to be precise
The sights and abridged partings
Abruptly tightening what's within phantoms
My world stopped, returning
When I heard a plane fly by, overhead
We on Earth, and us, here, in Hell's divisions,
levels and phases, trails and ends, raptures and
 beginnings – the wanderings of daylight
Behind the moments I recall, the noise before
 the coming, boundless freefall
Compare it, relate it, ignore it
Patching conversations, holding up the air
Suspension moves through this round's 'scape
Pushing back falling rocks

Honoring your Love

The clouds anchored the horizon and
through   to the sky, marbled over in
blues, whites and   purples,
oranges and yellows, greys spun, and
             everything is honest
  and nothing is true,
expect love, me and you.

What Kind?

What kind of hate do you have in your heart?
Is it for art and truth?
For Him or them?
Yourself even?
The other, your Lover or friends?
For what was or never did get said?
Your Mother or Kin?
For the powers at be or those that were and then?
What kind of hate do you have in your heart?
The fact that that never was, or perhaps, will be again?
For war or drugs? Or those that feel fine all the time?
That adults kill babies? Or that humans rape each other?
For revenge or bastard indifference?
For those wretched, disgusting other tribes?
Maybe yours mirrors mine?

Like I've been saying,
  what kind of hate do you have in your heart, my child,
    said all the Gods through <-> Time

Just

He didn't love drugs, he just was in love, loved
being in the end of such a when was not gone, or
at least under control, and so was the intake,
those people and the tolls, that which he
understood fully formed into the facts
that,

he didn't love drugs, he just loved not being in
pain

Today

He laughed,
 in bellows,
  like he had
   won the game
    Or at least realized
    he beat it
     today,
        nonetheless

Anyways

A quick wit reutterance of something better left said:

Like jumping through hoops that don't
 exist,

Complaining, since God's busy with your
 enemy's

   needs

Enjoyment

He chose otherwise
So, he enjoyed his Life
Vesting all but the absence of regret
A vacuum of beautiful blessings
Yielded the absence of nothing
A held truth to, parted gently, the repetition
 of breath and mornings, both like
        oh yeah
The death black spiral ended
In her joyful resistance to false freedom
Devoid of everything but their best Life

Painting Sonnets

Too good or too bad
Any way you cut it
It isn't appropriate

While trying to be good
He became the worst

So much for participating
　in opportunity of this lessness called
　　　　now living
Instead of respectable Life
Turbulent and of the tired
(Always) and anyway you cut it
The them cast out blame while holding a
downcast mirror, the light reflecting, regretting its
own shadow

With war, the we wages against the human in
men, the tortured and dead

We, like us, did that, this having no end,
　　　　like the child knowing,
　　　　like our own selves individually, weeping
and sorry, painting sonnets on the
　　　Sun
　　　　too good, to be too bad

You make your best pies with your
favorite ingredients :)

Symmetry

When you imagine the faults in creases
   of walls
And the heart that runs through
To corners of levels, high and true
Overcoming the lists of to-do's
Like the melodic stampede of just
   interludes
Between our two hearts, time, distance
   and you
When never saying, to me, anything but
I am
Because in the creases of walls
Lays the hints of Gods
In you, too

Me, too

money is not the root of all evil, but
  rather its means

My Exhaled Sum

The aftermath of the bar
Adjusts my perspective
On these quiet night dark streets
Juggling interpretations of the Divine and
Everything in between
Expect for the hum of passing cars
My exhaled sum
And the moving stars, above
Maybe just one blinking with my thoughts
Like the sidewalk lights and falling of leaves
Elevated in my way of bleeding, pleading,
Protection of right, sitting tight in the leaning of my
Healing and scarred,
Heart, stronger than the rest, and obliged
When forgiveness met the fight
And created sights steady, set and bravely whole,
Being in the center of my
Head's decision to keep going, the longing of a love song
Despite the fact that others hardly escape such a grip
Go, simply and justly fine,
Like, I want you to be here, with me, but
You're not able to now,
So, leave and let love, from where you are,
Go, simply and justly fine, so

Go and push your hands
Over and through the sky, the upward and
downfaced clouds, hard
Given the aftermath of booze and bars

Free Ways

Once he came Home
His name was resigned to freeways and
        underpasses
After he fell on the battle
Such is to say, live immediately
Not a rabbit hole, but rather a dove's flight

Rightly

His name was mentioned in a way no one
Regretted, but in their own self and
        choices to the best we could resign to do
Above underpasses and to free ways

That was his name

You can't stop the Wind

You can't stop the Wind, but you can
   certainly fly a kite,

So I let Love from where I am, and then I
understood, over and over again, that right,
 highly low and cheap like,

Sometimes you got to dance with the devil
 to change the Music, sights

Silence the ensued to the Beginning, an undoing
  of such sentiment, of nothing left, held faster
and bearing on cycles
   that never cease

 Below the hollow and shallow with fires and fears
of departing into solitude.

This easy pain and regret, just collecting,
collecting on a bet of making this
World a better place, nonetheLess :)

Clocks and Crosses

Reactions and obedience, mine of for a
   repeating hand
       and meaning tinted to tell everything
  including the truth
From some else
who gave a damn
just one

Like listening to shaded words'
                 wholeness
The first rapture's pass came fully past
Marking the cars' headlights reflecting
       under power lines and trees
            in hindsight on mirrors, too
Like a screaming, gently passing time
       with every go, leaf and bloom

   simple remembrance

  stood out trying these branches of blossoms
Like wows, promises and vows, yellows in
whites
This
    fright of days' night reverence
Coming back to

   like memories' (and oh, oh, the warmth)
      forgiveness
More than I could've handled
The release fell, cutting his face in half
 like our time here
   into edges and weeping hurt
But I do remember what we fought
     for and were
   below the although
 like me leaving all else above
 protecting the past never gave our future
      in doubt
Except every time across the coloring of
     clocks and crosses

The Acceptance of a Better Invitation

You don't have to be good to have a good life, was
said slyly.
Something like a lie struck him seductively, built
on things and parted pleasures, leaving his love
behind our will to survive, coming and staying
heart over.
Except the true recollections on humans,
lifting her to the one of these done sums, settling.
You overcame love to find living, forgetting
stillness and belief in these
complicated and steady deeds,
beyond hope and need, rather than Being.
So, like it's said, you don't have to be good, to
have a good life.
But when it is rather in freedom and decency,
such actions invite betterment and sweetness,
honoring the Gods and then some

Worthful Wonder

After acknowledging my tribe, the diatribes
disappeared into pretty pity,
along belonging by
free fought thought, flights and heights,
grit and gumption, easy like, blending into buena
ondas, when good waves rise
over, and over again, that there
sorrowful bigotry and hateful regret,
dwarfed and irrelevant, as being one of many,
riding high and hopeful, like
silk waves on strong water, priced by proud
decisions towards right, us,
rewarded in worthful wonder,
dazzling in delight.

That there

Never been to win
or figure out finally
But rather
to live
freely and fully
a
Life

So

He shamed God with his anger and sorrow
Again and again, no matter what was held by or said
Again and again
His sorrow and anger becomes none, nothing but an emptiness and dread
And then is something overflowing, overcome
Shaming God with your anger, sorrow and dread
Breaks along the horizon to show you
Again and again
Such things just bring love, love and loves from above
Honoring through belief,
and moreover actions done,
no matter what,
so

As with speaking with the Stars

The poets, who are good,
translate the divine for
humankind, humbly
and with
truth telling.

Amongst

Our upside-down and backwards flag
Darkened faith abounding in a meddling media a
way away from close community
Inversely spoken, these untruths
Holding our smothered mouths and hearts
Scared and timidly accepting
the absence of colors
In its place, placating patriotism rises in the void
of humans standing up for us
The suck of decency amongst our depths
over into silence witnessing our own undoings
The ease of bigotry tricks me steadily
That sly bastard
And you too, the right, the middle and left, our us
eroding into
indifference to beauty and life, each of ours
So, each morning, night and day
despite my regular failings and shortcomings
I do stand up
amongst white roses and steel petals
of our human bests
to the wind and next
because we're worth the present fight
to better tomorrow

In the Mirror

They threw it right in my face
They threw it right in my face!

(But I)

I smelled it
I heard it flying
Right in my face
And I saw it with my own eyes!

(Those goddamn sides of God I don't like)

(Those sides of God)

Goddammit!

Afterwards, and after I came to all my senses, I understood this to be what I can't stand to see in the mirror, those shifting sides and misunderstood pleadings, I couldn't stand in me at all, then

That there for you

God is so good and most merciful,
patient and true

But what about your you
as like my me

On our own and letting go
to understand this

That God is such a good and most merciful
love in my heart,
an all-encompassing that there

But what about my me like your you?

The suck of hollow, remembering

This here, rest of peace – whatever that means, yet,
what rest in peace was, just old enough

to grip and release this understanding

of here life, these feelings

like the drink and ease of mouth,

understanding words spent, sent and such

a worthless judgment from them,

like drinking from an empty glass,

in the right surroundings when

it gave you sight

   to see inside all that rest

 of peace, which I mean

to find and understand,

was what I told you in a far-a-way

      here to there,

    resting in peace, finally meaning home,

these feelings and, like the suck of hollow,

remembering

    that I hope life treats you good and well, like afterwards

Not again, but now

Dwell on the impermanence of now, for it is all you'll have in the end when time becomes something you can't stand by or command, seizing forgetfulness ahead of laying it down alone, as in the end, the power of walking, deliberately, away from the impermanence of now, dwelling on you holding with me, not again, but now

You Alone

And I will be alone in providence,
  walking with the Lord,
    amongst the absence of nothing.

For, I don't have to imagine, but be,

  humbly and with truth telling.

Well beyond wealth, and comforted beyond

    contented, alone and in faith,

I am born, again, to say,

I don't have to imagine

    but be and walk all with the Lord,

  amongst many

Home

I grew up when I realized dying meant

    going home,

  in due time, not now – thank God! – but when

    after words become unsung into

  this here now bliss

lasts longer than history goes, the closer to the gods

we get, not yet, but soon

Laughing Beautifully

The endless night or the daymares of life

What breaks you beyond repair?

Keep your faith, and build your belonging to

how your essence is, and with the spirits, too, fully

all by claiming yourself completely, deserving
from love of above and here to there by

making no mistake that a fear of freedom is a gift
from the grotesque, bound to no thing decently,

so know what you belong to, and feel the freedom
in faith of this here and then when, in our endless
nights, dreams are way beyond such
comprehension, laughing beautifully

He ___ thought

Since the height

of faith is the rise

of harmony when

the music is nothing, but

everything gone and too plainly seen,

after seeing too much, so

that's what he though, ____ anyways.

– my God is friends with your God –

You try to save the world, you'll lose yourself

You try to save yourself, you'll gain the world

This here Life

    I passed on the wisdom from this and gave the woe to God.

He'd pat his eyes, and then it'd come from his nose or mouth, 'cause it really, and truth be told, never really stopped coming, like I belonged to evermore true, 'cause I never stopped, like

I know everything will get better, but

    I chose to absolve the guilt, and guilty, so you'd stop crying, for once, or twice, 'cause the case for you only goes along remembering. Remember you. Along, remembering the decision to leave right now or let life die this way, this here life,

        is up to you!

...your deeds and doings decide your decency...

Remember, we are guests here

Dedicated to humans,
              hope
   and pizza.

Thanks to my friends and family, who called me home despite the horrors of my heart, and said then, in due time, build your own

```
        F
        R
    L I E B E
        I
        H
        E
        I
        T
```

www.ingramcontent.com/pod-product-compliance
Lightning Source LLC
Chambersburg PA
CBHW022115040426
42450CB00006B/708